W9-AFB-103

WITHDRAWN

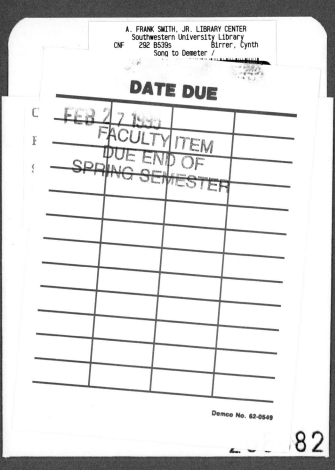

82

SONG TO
DEMETER

TOLD AND ILLUSTRATED BY
CYNTHIA AND WILLIAM BIRRER

LOTHROP, LEE & SHEPARD BOOKS
NEW YORK

FOR PHYLLIS

NOTE   The ancient Greeks believed in a family of gods and goddesses who controlled all that happened in the universe. Many of their stories explain the natural world. This story is the ancient Greek explanation for the seasons of the year. The gods and goddesses who appear here are: Zeus, king of all the gods; Demeter, goddess of the harvest; Persephone, daughter of Demeter and wife of Pluto; Pluto, god of the underworld and the dead.

The illustrations are machine-stitched appliqué and embroidery on fabric.

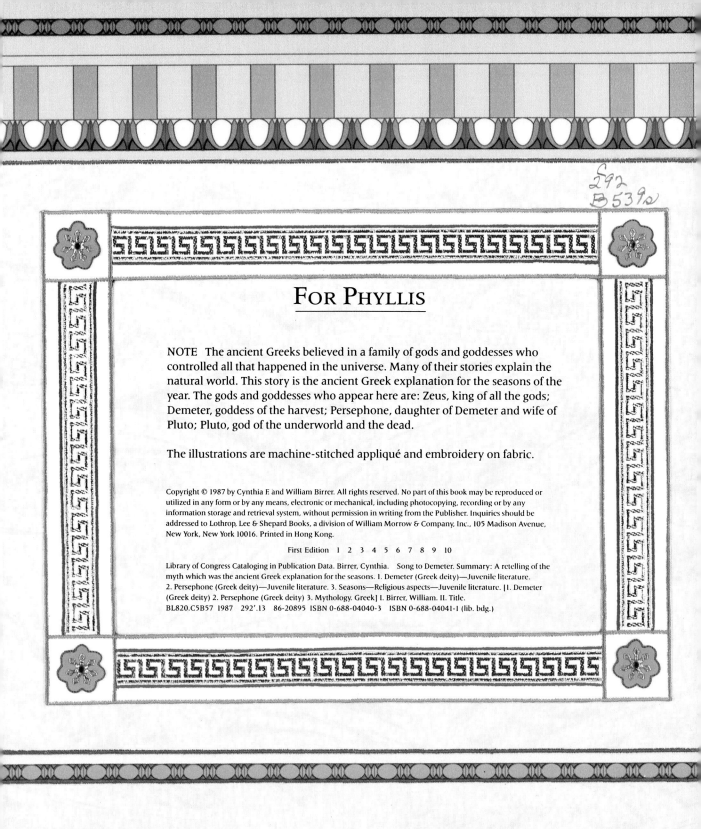

Demeter was the goddess of the harvest. All year she watched over the earth, causing it to bring forth fruit. Demeter had a beautiful young daughter, Persephone, whom she loved dearly.

Demeter's brother, Pluto, also loved Persephone. One day, he thundered up from his home in the underworld and swept her away with him in his golden chariot.

He took her down to the darkness of Hades, where he was king. Beautiful Persephone, a child of sunshine, became queen of the kingdom of the dead.

When Demeter discovered that Persephone was missing, she disguised herself as an old woman and wandered far and wide, searching for her daughter.

Demeter's grief was so great she thought her heart
would break. After many days of searching in vain, she
met some village women, who took pity on her.

The women took her to their king, who recognized the goddess and welcomed her to his household. He asked her to tell them the reason for her great sadness.

The king's eldest son overheard Demeter's story, and
told of having seen a beautiful young girl and a man in
a golden chariot fly down into the earth and disappear.

Demeter knew that the man in the chariot could only be
Pluto, and that he must have taken Persephone to the underworld. Demeter's grief turned to anger. As her anger increased,
the earth grew cold. Plants withered and animals died.

A terrible hunger spread throughout the land. When
Zeus learned the cause of the suffering, he became
worried that the people too would soon die. He
summoned Demeter to Mount Olympus.

Zeus sent a messenger to Pluto to tell him that he must return Persephone at once. He then made a promise to Demeter.

Persephone could live with Demeter always, but on one condition: She must not have eaten the food of Hades during her stay there.

Pluto listened to the message from Zeus, and at first was angry. But when he heard Zeus's promise, his anger turned to cunning determination that he would have his way.

He ordered his servant to take Persephone to her
mother at once. Then he sent Persephone four seeds
from a pomegranate and told her to eat them to give
her strength for the journey.

After many long months in the underworld, Persephone
was overjoyed that she would see her mother again.

As she and the messenger flew across the sky,
Persephone ate the seeds that Pluto had given her.

Demeter and Persephone greeted each other with a loving embrace. Demeter's heart was brimming with happiness,

and she asked Persephone to tell everything that had
happened to her since Pluto had taken her away.

Her happiness vanished when Persephone mentioned the
pomegranate seeds and revealed that she had eaten them.

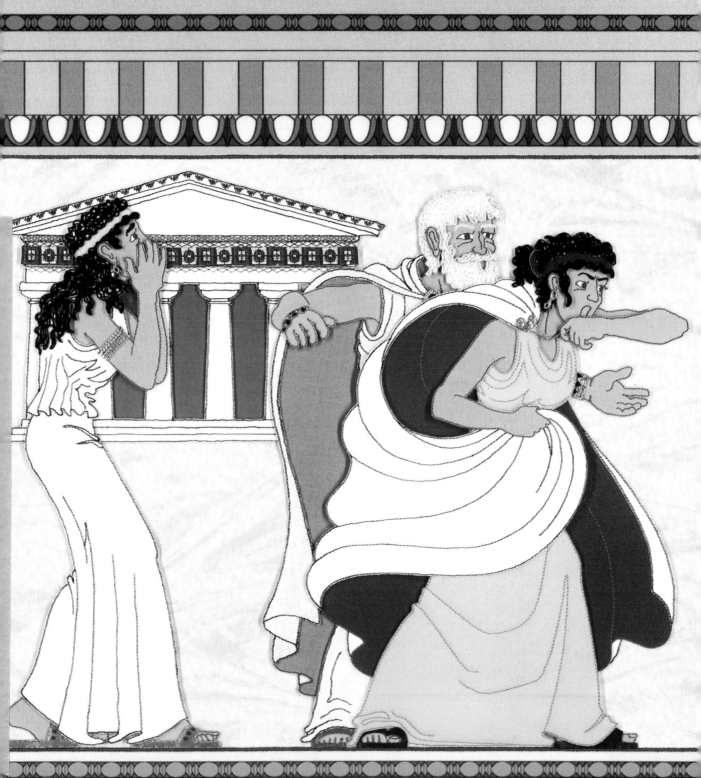

In despair, Demeter refused to lift the curse from the
land, unless Persephone could remain by her side.

Zeus could not go back on his promise, but to save the earth he declared that Persephone would live with Pluto four months, one for each of the pomegranate seeds she had eaten;

and she would live with Demeter the other eight
months of the year. Demeter promised that the sun
would return and the earth would be green when
Persephone was with her.

Each year after that, when Persephone visited the
underworld,

Demeter and the people mourned and the world was cold and gray.

Persephone's return brought joy to all.

Everything blossomed and flourished.

The earth became green and beautiful.

Fruits ripened and grain was plentiful.

As the time for Persephone's departure neared,

trees shed their leaves in sorrow and the grass withered.

So were born the seasons. Buds of spring follow
winter's bleakness, and summer's fullness fades to fall.